Melancholic Happiness

Lachlan Lamey

BookLeaf Publishing

Presentation by *BookLeaf Publishing*

Web: www.bookleafpub.com

E-mail: info@bookleafpub.com

ISBN: 9789357212274

First edition 2023

DEDICATION

I'd like to dedicate this book to my family, who are the most supportive people in my life. Mum, Dad, Kass, and Bro, thank you for being in my life and helping me pursue my dreams.

PREFACE

Reader beware you are in for not a scare, but depression. An omnibus of emotionally driven dribble straight from the mouth of an autistic, depressed, nerd who likes to think that he can do things with words that make them sound good.

To put it in words that aren't so self-depreciating, I write with my heart and soul and while I might not always think what I write is good, I've been told it's tolerable. I've had people look me directly in the face and say "Lachlan, that was a good poem." and I've had to nod along and believe them because if I didn't it would cause a whole conversation, and talking to people isn't really my thing.

The overarching theme is that there is no overarching theme. A perfect reflection of my inner thoughts as I struggle to keep track of my emotions, one poem makes me cry, the next one makes me laugh. It all blends together into some amalgamation of words that I can't really describe, it makes no sense, has no order. I feel as though that having these poems not really have anything connecting them (except for poems 10 & 11) makes it that much more my style.

So to whoever is reading this, please enjoy a journey through my mind. Complete with a complementary serving of mental illness and a touch of personal insanity.

The Corvid Calls

The corvid calls
A beacon to show his kin
Fresh seeds and fruits are near
All thanks to him
A murder of his brethren swarm
Picking the trees bare
Leaving none for the one
Who called them there

The corvid calls
All he does, he does for love
A mating call echoes
Through the trees above
Other calls mix with his
Mates flock to their source
But one call never gets traced
It's his, of course

The corvid calls
Desperate for assistance
A brother is wounded
Low on perseverance
Their death is imminent
But no help arrives
All that surrounds them are giant metal creatures
With their bright shining eyes

The corvid calls
For what he's not sure
He just hopes for someone
To give his loneliness a cure
But no corvid responds
There are no replies
No one cares to notice him
The corvid cries

The Crossroads

The full moon illuminates
An empty stretch of road
A dirt path crossing through
Far from any postal code

My car is long behind me
My mind is full of doubt
But still I'm here at midnight
To see what the fuss is about

They say that at the crossroads
You meet a simple man
He who will give you anything
Where many a career began

But like everything in life
It comes at a price
For when you meet your end
You become a sacrifice

You lend your soul for power
Money or even fame
Yet all he sees are fools
To him we're all the same

I’ve been here for an hour
I knew it wasn’t true
Selling your soul to a devil
So people can idolise you

I turn around in frustration
To return the way I came
Of course this isn’t the way
For me to find my fame

But as I leave the crossroads
Knowing now what is real
A man in a suit appears behind me
And asks me to make a deal

Cracked Reflection

I look in the mirror
My face stares back at me
But which face is reflecting
Through the glass portal

The mirror cracks
My face shatters into pieces
Each one representing a mask
That I wear to fool others

There's the largest piece
The normal average person
Going about their day like nothing is wrong
But this piece breaks too easily

The other pieces vary
In size and meaning
Each piece a split off of the main mask
To make certain people not hate me

I morph my interests and dislikes
To fit in with the crowd I find myself in
Pretend to change the way I view the world
For another 5 minutes of false comradery

The mirror falls apart
The glass littering the floor
All that remains is one tiny speck
My true face that no one else sees

While it still shows my face to me
Like all the other pieces do
It's so small I can hardly make out
What makes this one different

What makes me who I am
When can I take of the masks
Why do I have to conform to these unspoken rules
Of communication and body language

The mirror reforms
The cracks conceal themselves
The one reflection that stands before me
Is just as confused as I am

Duck

The image of a duck on water
Is such a calming sight
But no one stops to think
About it's internal plight

For you see, on the surface
The duck is calm and free
But beneath the calm, it struggles
And it perfectly mirrors me

Because like a duck
I'm told I look calm, but take a closer look
And you'll see all the struggles
That plague the pages of my book

But unlike a duck
Who's struggle is in its feet
That move with the power
Of an entire naval fleet

My struggle is internal
It comes from inside
The overwhelming desire
To just run and hide

Anxiety is a pain
I'll give that one for free
Functioning is hard
When most people can scare me

But my struggle is not as bad
As the duck's, hands down
For if the duck would stop kicking
There's the chance it might drown

But we both are similar
Motivated by our fear
But that big key difference
Makes everything clear

So next time you feel
Like your all out of luck
Just imagine yourself
As a little yellow duck

Why must they fight?

Steel clashes with steel
In a beautiful dance of death
Two warriors locked in battle
Until one draws their final breath

These two armoured fighters
Wielding blades of shining steel
A lifetime trained for battle
For fighting with aggressive zeal

There are hundreds just like them
Fighting alongside each other
But both sides are growing smaller
With one death after another

But these two warriors suddenly cease
Fighting for their lives
They stop to look around
As their brothers-in-arms dies

The two soldiers lock eyes
They both begin to doubt
Why they're even here to begin with
What this battle is all about

What is it that they fight for
Honour? Power? Fame?
Maybe they just want to rid
Themselves of inner shame

Other fighters begin to share
This sudden surge of thought
All over the battlefield
They realise that all is for naught

Weapons start to fall
Dropped by the warriors hand
They fall near the bodies
Strewn about the blood-stained sand

In that moment there is peace
As the two armies realise
What point is there in victory
If it costs so many lives

A tale of a bee

There once was a little striped bee
Who heard a tale of an ethnic flea
They shared the same passion
Of a musical fashion
He said "hey that could be me"

So he got up and left his hive
As he wasn't a fan of their jive
He flew through the cities
While humming his ditties
So that he could go and perform them live

Around a week or two later
He'd made it way past the equator
The other hemisphere
Was his new musical frontier
As long as he didn't need a translator

The bee was dreaming of praise
That he'd get from the music he plays
But no one would hear his sound
As he dropped to the ground
Because bees only live 30 days

A soldier's duty

I am a soldier
Enlisted to fight in war
For the glory of my country, I give my life
My gear has no equal, I am the best I can be
Fighting those who stand to oppose us
Drones cover me from the sky as my team clear the streets
NVG's illuminate what our enemy can't see
I fight to protect my home

I am a soldier
Drafted to fight in war
My nation is losing, yet I'm forced to give my life
The smell of napalm fills the air as the surroundings burn to ash
Given the bare minimum to fight against our foes
We barely know the terrain, while our enemies hide in the trees
They'll ambush us, provided we don't trigger their traps first
I just want this to be over so I can go home

I am a soldier

Fighting in the war
The landing craft barely made it to the beach
Before half of my squad was torn to shreds
I'm barely halfway through high school
Yet enlisted to fight on the front lines
Explosions, gunshots, and garand pings drown out my thoughts
I should've stayed at home

I am a soldier
Fighting the great war
I fell for the lies told to me
They said the war would end by christmas
But they didn't say which one
The gas floods my trench, I affix my mask
If I survive today, tomorrow I go over the top
I'm not going to make it home

I am a soldier
Enlisted in the war
For the freedom of my nation, I give my life
Fighting back our oppressors
The cannon fire shakes the earth
My musket shakes in my hand
But I'll willingly die for my cause
I fight to protect my home

Four Thieves

Once there was a band of four thieves
Each had a cowl to hide their face
They would strike at midnight
Taking all, not leaving a trace

They did the bidding of kings
And revolutionaries alike
They worked for whomever paid them
They didn't care about what was right

But after a job went south
And one of them lost his head
The other three parted ways
So they wouldn't all end up dead

For a few years they hid
Laying low, biding their time
For when they would be needed
For when there was a lull in crime

The thieves emerged again
A replacement filled their ranks
The team of four struck back
Against the one that got their friend killed, the banks

The four thieves stole their way
Around the world and back again
Then faded into legend
After their robbery campaign

Decades turned to centuries
And memories began to fade
The thieves no longer mattered
Their legend had decayed

But four men of different paths
Met a man who knew a way
To bring back legends of past
It was time for a payday

Sleep

I hate going to bed
I never want to sleep
I always end up uncomfortable
Tangled up in my sheets

My back always hurts
My neck always aches
The bed springs pierce the mattress
Taking bits of skin in flakes

My mind just won't calm down
Rushing thoughts won't cease
Counting sheep won't help
My mind find it's peace

My eyes feel so heavy
I yawn every second
My whole body is heavy
As my slumber beckons

Sleeping is a pain
A physical and mental headache
But the worst part about going to bed
Is knowing that tomorrow I will awake

The village

Another day in our peaceful village
They all blur in my mind
The countless days working the fields
These are quiet and simple days

I wipe the sweat from my brow
Wheat, corn, potatoes all harvested for our lands
Wool and fleece protect my skin from the elements
My family and I are safe here as we live our lives

I see a distant traveller
Clad in black robes and a wide brimmed hat
He's writing something down
He lifts his head from his book and I see his mask

It's one of them, those doctors
Where they go, sickness follows
They are the bringers of death
These bird-faced reapers of life

My wife cries as she hugs our children
My father just lets out a sigh

All I can do is stare into that mask of his
These monsters were meant to keep the illness away from us

Why must he have come here
Bringing his death and disease
The doctors are no help to us
Our only salvation is death

The doctor

Another day, another village
They all blur in my mind
The fearful townsfolk strewn among the corpse
filled streets
This is the end of days

My mask keeps me safe from the miasma of
death
Herbs, flowers, and cloves filter away the smell
Oiled leather keeps the pestilence off of my
hands
I am protected while I go about my research

I open my notebook, take down the name on the
sign
And mentally prepare myself for what's to come
Expecting to see rows of corpses, people
surrounded by fear
Death enveloping them in it's gaping maw

Yet opening my eyes I see not a nightmare but a
dream
The people going about their day as if hell isn't
approaching

Yet as I become noticed the townsfolk mood shifts
The normalcy has ceased because of me

A mother cries as she hugs her children
An elderly man bows his head in silence
This village is now aware of the sickness's spread
And the madness that follows with it

Why must I have been the first one sent here
The one to bring this depressing reality
All that I can do is hang my head in shame
And try not to break completely as I speak

"I'm sorry."

Staring at the screen

Night after night is the same boring sight
My monitor illuminating my room in pale white
I can't shake the feeling, try as I might
It's just my brain's way of telling me I'm not
alright

The glare hurts my eyes
As companies advertise
While I scroll through countless lies
From those whom I despise

But in between the media binge, I just stare
Contemplating why I'm even there
I'd message someone, would they even care
But now my back hurts from sitting in my chair

I stop staring at the screen, now I stare within
Searching my own self, all the places I've been
And how they all circle back to where it would
begin
Being nothing more than a lonely shut-in

This has become my nightly routine
For when I'm all out of dopamine
Yet my rational side reminds me how obscene
It is to blankly stare at my computer screen

Don't wake the sleeping bear

Tip toe, tip toe
Don’t wake the sleeping bear
It’ll rip your throat out
Don’t get close, don’t you dare

Just keep your mouth shut
And watch where you tread
Only breathe when you feel safe enough
Lest the ground run red

Make it past the slaughter
And you will find your peace
Only to trip on a twig
And find death’s release

The bear doesn’t need a reason
To want to see you dead
You dared to get too close to it
Not listening to what others said

They warned you not to speak
Told you to hold your tongue
But you just had to open your mouth
So from your entrails you’ll be hung

You become another warning
Shown outside the beast’s lair
Hopefully people learn soon
To not wake the sleeping bear

The great emu war

There was a war fought long ago
Against a rather peculiar foe
The enemy was not a nation
Or some radical organisation
But rather something stopping crops grow

In the state of Australia's west
There was an increase in a certain pest
Those blasted emus
Breaking fences and getting through
Eating all the wheat, leaving farmers stressed

So the locals called the army for troops
To get rid of these emu nincompoops
Two blokes with a Lewis gun each
Found the emus too far out of reach
And they were too fast and in too small of groups

They next tried an ambush at a dam
Our heroes McMurray and O'Halloran
Waited for them to get close
A thousand birds they would dispose
If their guns didn't up and bloody jam

Six days and 2,500 rounds later

Only 50 birds had met their maker
So they had to withdraw
That was the last straw
They probably hadn’t saved a single acre

5 days passed and the farmers asked
For help with these emus, and fast
The heat and drought bring them in
They don’t stop when they begin
There’s barely enough wheat, we’re aghast

So again the soldiers arrived
To cull these birds they had grown to despise
They’d kill 100 per week
But the situation was still bleak
Because too many of them survived

So in the end they just had to cease
Because the emu population wouldn't
decrease
With them going gung ho
They wasted so much ammo
But at least they saved some of the wheat

So that was the great emu war
An amusing tale for sure
In the end we had lost
And it would come at the cost
Of being made fun of forever more

Perfect Love

There is a woman who loves me
Who can accept me for who I am
My endless flaws she doesn't mind
My countless failures she doesn't care

She respects me for my humour
I respect her for her understanding
She makes me feel like I'm alright
Like there's nothing to worry about

We share each other's interests
We agree on most points
We think alike, talk alike, walk alike
Two peas in a pod we thrive

Her eyes are like portals to another dimension
A place of peace a tranquillity
I get lost in them so much I never want to leave
Yet she brings me back to reality with her kiss

She means the world to me
Our love is stronger than steel
I'd go to hell and back four times over
Just to see her smile

This woman is perfection
Or as close as I can get to it
True love, happiness, companionship
How I wish she was real

Magnet

A magnet in a metal river
Where it lies is completely dry
The river flows around it
It doesn't fit, it doesn't attract
It sits there motionless
While other magnets pass it by
Mingling with the endless steel

The magnet starts to move
The metal starts to part
Wherever the magnet goes
The steel doesn't wish to be
Actively ignoring
Trying not to coexist
With something foreign to it

It doesn't matter what happens
The magnet just can't attract anything
It's polarity is just incompatible
With its surroundings
How do all the other magnets connect
With the flow of engulfing metal
It's lonely here when everything just doesn't
want to be near

Labyrinth

I'm completely lost in here
I can not find my path
Who even designed this place
Some twisted psychopath

The endless branching paths
Only lead me to dead ends
The walls all look so similar
In my mind they all just blend

I stop for just a moment
But something catches my ear
The sound of stones moving
What was far has now become near

This maze is forever shifting
Always changing its face
And because of its constant moving
I'll never get out of this place

I have no light to guide me
Only my sense of worth
But once that runs out
I'll just collapse in the dirt

How long have I been here
How many paths have I tried
Will I ever get the chance to escape
The labyrinth that is my mind

Orca

Oh how calming is the ocean
It's fields of infinite blue
The countless creatures all living beneath
The surface of an aqua hue

Are you seeing what I see
A dorsal fin breaches the waves
Though the creature isn't a shark
It still has sent many creatures to their graves

See now the black and white
The pattern of it's skin
The majestically beautiful orca
The largest of dolphin kin

A killer whale as some call them
Their tactics rival that of MI6
They flank, ambush, and communicate
To send prey to the river styx

The orca is perceived as a killer
Ruthless and unforgiving
While that is true to some end
They really are just living

Any time an orca attacks us
Is when it is a captive
Made to jump for our amusement
At least with that it's active

The orca can be a sad creature
Cursed with such intelligence
To understand that you can't go back home
And only dance for the ignorant

Yet seeing an orca in the wild
Is such an amazing sight to behold
To see one breach the dark blue ocean
Is worth its weight in gold

The axe forgets

The axe is grinded sharp to cut
The tree just stands there still
What it did wrong? The tree doesn't know what.
But the axe still gets it's kill

Words can cut sharper than any axe
But feelings are as tough as a tree
They think it's all just meaningless acts
When they say those things to me

But much like the axe, after time passes by
They forget the wounds they make
Yet the tree remembers everything, no matter
how hard it tries
Everything from it that they just had to take

Every tree is different
From their strength to their height
But every axe can be ignorant
Believing what it does it right

I'll never forget the axes I've faced
All the cuts and wounds they made
And the memories for them are all erased
While my scars take forever to fade

Sky Dragons

A simple thing flying high
Made of condensed vapor and ice
They litter the sky, only to leave with the wind
Clouds, the cotton wool clumps of a beautiful
day.

They make the imagination run wild
Like a hamster in its wheel
Seeing images in the shapes
Makes for great inspiration.

My mind sees a dog, a fish, a pig
A gap in the clouds looks like an eye, the sun
shining through the center
That small amalgamation of shapes resembles a
mascot
Of that brand whose name I can't remember.

Yet outshining them all is a legend
A great fantastical beast
From its scales all the way down to its tail
The dragon, is what I see

Is it a dragon from the east?
Wise as his tail is long

Bringing wisdom, advice and good fortune
Perhaps warning of an oncoming storm.

Or is it a Dragon from the west?
Tyrannical, menacing and feared,
Spewing fire from his mouth to cleanse all he deems unworthy
Only to return to his cave of wealth.

Maybe it's not even a dragon
But rather a drake or even a wyvern
It all comes down to the number of legs it has
Nobody cares to tell the difference these days

But still, the dragons watch over
From morning to dusk they loom over the horizon
Moving with the clouds that shape them
Their journey never to end

The clouds can tell so many tales
So much that sticks in our brain
But in the end, we're seeing things where there isn't anything
Pareidolia, it fuels the imagination.

Melancholic Happiness

A melancholic happiness
An oxymoron, contradictory
How can a thing of sorrow
Contain any amount of joy

An artist reflects on their work
Contempt at the very least
They could change everything now
Or just be happy it's complete

They hate their own art
Yet others seem to applaud
The creations are acceptable
Even if they are somewhat flawed

The artist doesn't know
How to work with a smile
If they are aware of it or not
It still affects their artistic style

But when told by the people
That the work makes them feel
The realization of the artist's own joy
Just feels too unreal

They create when they're down
To lift up other spirits
Their melancholy results
In some form of happiness

www.ingramcontent.com/pod-product-compliance
Lightning Source LLC
Chambersburg PA
CBHW051744130826
49812CB00033B/1001
9789357212274